# AS Ethics

*Revision Guide for OCR*

Peter Baron

# Contents

# Acknowledgment

I am grateful to Henry Swales for permission to include in this guide original material from his revision summary sheets first developed for his students at Tonbridge School, Kent.

# Introduction to Ethics

## NORMATIVE ETHICS

Asks the question "how should I act, morally speaking?" or "what ought I to do?"

A norm is a "value", meaning "something I think of as good" The normative theories we study at AS (OCR) are: Relativism, Natural Law, Kantian Ethics, Utilitarianism and Christian Ethics.

Note: Christian Ethics is Situation Ethics, Natural Law theory and Divine Command.

## META-ETHICS

Meta-ethics concerns the nature and meaning of ethics (what does it mean to say something is good?). It particularly focuses on ethical language. Meta-ethics is studied at **A2** level. A key meta-ethical question is:

> *"Is morality absolute – applying everywhere and for all time, or is it relative, specific to a time and place – a culture, situation or viewpoint?"*

# APPLIED ETHICS

Applies ethical theories to real world situations. The applied issues at AS (OCR) are:

- **Abortion**

- **Euthanasia**

- **War and peace**

- **Genetic Engineering**

- **IVF and right to a child**

# DEONTOLOGICAL

Acts are right or wrong in themselves (intrinsically) – it is not about consequences. Often stresses the rules or duties (Kant, Natural Law, Divine Command Theory). **DEON** is Greek for duty.

# TELEOLOGICAL

Teleological theories (telos = end in Greek) focuses on consequences of actions. An action is good only if it brings about beneficial consequences (it is instrumentally good, not intrinsically because actions are means to some other end like happiness or pleasure), for example, Utilitarianism and Situation ethics.

Four questions to ask of moral theories:

- **DERIVATION** - How does the moral theory derive (produce) the idea of goodness?

- **APPLICATION** - How can we apply the "good" to choices we make?

- **REALISM** - How realistic is the theory?

- **MOTIVATION** - Why should I be moral?

These questions will be answered for all moral theories in the final chapter.

# Moral Relativism

Relativism implies either that the meaning of "good" is relative to a particular culture, **CULTURAL RELATIVISM**, or that there is no universal, objective **NORM** or value against which we can judge different claims: **NORMATIVE RELATIVISM**. So someone could make an **ABSOLUTE** claim – true for their own tribe, society or culture, (eg "stealing is always wrong"), but if another culture disagrees ("stealing is sometimes ok – it depends") we have no way of deciding who is right. Normative relativism doesn't stop you being an absolutist – but you are an absolutist who says "I have no way of proving my absolutism is right."

## KEY TERMS

- **RELATIVISM** - the view that there are no objective moral truths – values depend on culture, choice or situation.

- **CULTURAL RELATIVISM** – the view that cultures generate different values – a descriptive view of morals.

- **NORMATIVE RELATIVISM** – the view that there can never be such a thing as objective truth – norms are generated by different habits, behaviours and belief systems.

- **OBJECTIVE TRUTH** – the view that truth is testable by observation and experience.

- **SUBJECTIVE TRUTH** – the view that truth is something that depends on an individual perception or belief system and cannot be shared objectively.

- **SITUATION ETHICS** – a theory of ethics that holds that what is good or bad needs to be assessed according to what maximises love in any situation.

- **AGAPE LOVE** – the highest of the four loves in Greek ethics involving sacrificial love for a stranger.

- **TELEOLOGICAL ETHICS** – ethics that focuses on the end or telos of an action, for example, Situation Ethics focuses on love as the highest end or purpose.

- **DEONTOLOGICAL ETHICS** – ethics that focuses on the duty (deon) or rule.

- **DEPENDENCY THESIS** – the view of some relativists that norms depend on culture and beliefs.

- **DIVERSITY THESIS** – the view that cultures are always different and so as a description of the real world, cultural values always differ.

## TRIBAL CULTURES

Eskimos kill the elderly because food is short in winter; Spartans killed babies judged "weak"; Aboriginal tribes had no concept of the biological parents as children belong to the tribe. So Ruth **BENEDICT** argues moral values are just **SOCIALLY APPROVED HABITS**. As societies change and develop so values of right and wrong change and if we compare two different societies today, in one (Ireland) abortion is equivalent to murder, and in another (Britain) abortion is permitted under certain legal conditions (eg up to 24 weeks). Ireland is influenced by **CATHOLIC** thinking, and Britain by **PROTESTANT** liberalism. We have no **OBJECTIVE** standard for judging which is "right". We agree to disagree.

## JL MACKIE'S ARGUMENT

Mackie argues that values emerge out of **FORMS OF LIFE**. These are beliefs, habits, patterns of behaviour which determine what is approved as "right" and what is approved as "wrong". These may be religious in origin (as above) or secular – driven for example by human rights or an understanding, from science, that gay people are genetically different. **FORMS OF LIFE** change before **VALUES** change. So in WWII women started to fly planes, drive lorries and boats, farm, and do other jobs traditionally associated with men. The old argument that they were unsuited to such things had to change as a result of this experience. So **EQUALITY** gained momentum and eventually, in 1975, it became **ILLEGAL** to discriminate on grounds of gender. Or consider how **CONTRACEPTION** in the 1960s changed **SEXUAL ETHICS** (JL MACKIE, Inventing Right and Wrong).

## JAMES RACHELS' ARGUMENT

James **RACHELS** argues that **MACKIE** makes a logical error here, because when he says "there are no **OBJECTIVE** truths", this is itself an **ABSOLUTE** statement. A **RELATIVIST** ends up with an **ABSOLUTE** conclusion. How can we possibly know? Secondly, we need to look at the **EVIDENCE** for objective values. When Colin **TURNBULL** studied the IK tribe in Kenya, he noticed values such as cruelty to the elderly, extreme selfishness in food distribution, scorn for the weak – but also the tribe was **DISINTEGRATING**. So...if we don't share some common **OBJECTIVE** values eg respect for life, compassion, co-operation the human race will not **FLOURISH**. We have established an objective test for goodness. We can also ask, why is it that some principles like the **GOLDEN RULE** "do as you would be done by" can be found in all ethical systems and religions? Go to the Golden Rule website for a full list. Admittedly this is a **NATURALISTIC** argument some would reject – that goodness can be observed in some **NATURAL FEATURE** of the world, or humanity, such as Richard **DAWKINS** who argues for an genetically programmed, evolved "**LUST** to be **NICE**" or altruistic gene.

## SITUATION ETHICS

According to **FLETCHER** situation ethics is a relativist theory because there are no **ABSOLUTE** rules which hold true **ALWAYS**. We should break any rule if **AGAPE** love demands it. So technically there is one absolute, **UNCONDITIONAL** love. But everything needs to be made **RELATIVE** to this principle, and the **SITUATION** – we don't know the right thing to do until we experience the situation – hence **SITUATION ETHICS**. Richard **JACOBS** calls this "**PRINCIPLED RELATIVISM**" – because situation ethics and **UTILITARIANISM** do have one absolute **VALUE** (love, happiness), but a. What this value means differs from age to age, culture to culture (look how **LOVE** has changed its meaning), and b. Everything has to be measured according to this value, including things like stealing, lying, promise-keeping (traditional examples of **ABSOLUTES**).

## ATTACKS ON RELATIVISM

Relativism is a feature of **POSTMODERN** society which sees **PLURALISM** as an intrinsic good. We are judged by the norm of **TOLERANCE** (but should we tolerate torture? Genocide? Racism?). **EXPERIENCE** comes before principle. We pick and mix between

16

different **WORLDVIEWS**. Reason itself is **CULTURAL** – eg a Buddhist tends to argue that **TRUTH** lies in **PARADOX**, whereas the **ENLIGHTENMENT** (16th – 19th century) philosophers like **KANT** follow Aristotelean **LOGIC** such as the principle that something cannot be and not be at the same time (the principle of **NON-CONTRADICTION**). The attack on relativism can be **SECULAR**, for example, those who argue for **UNIVERSAL HUMAN RIGHTS** derived from common human values, and **RELIGIOUS**, such as Pope **BENEDICT** who speaks of "the tyranny of relativism" and calls for a return to **OBJECTIVE** values. Ironically by placing the **AUTONOMOUS INDIVIDUAL** at the centre, the **REFORMATION** opened the way for the individual to make up his or her own values.

## STRENGTHS

Relativism breeds **RESPECT** for others and **TOLERATION** of differences. Other **RELIGIONS** are no longer branded **INFIDEL** as in the Anglican **39 ARTICLES** of belief. **PREJUDICE** may be replaced with **UNDERSTANDING** and genuine **CONVERSATION** – where "a conversation implies the possibility of conversion to the other's point of view" (Alasdair MacIntyre). Traditional practices such as women staying at home change not because of **RELIGION** (women were ordained priests only in 1993 and still can't be Bishops), but **REASON** challenging stereotypical views. Morality becomes **PROGRESSIVE** rather than stagnant, adapting to our times.

## WEAKNESSES

How can there be **MORAL PROGRESS** when we can't judge what is **BETTER**? So the idea of a **BETTER WORLD** implies some **OBJECTIVE** testable idea about what would be **GOOD** (eg no pollution, no racism, no war). We cannot **CONDEMN** someone for holding a view such as "genocide is good" or "women are inferior" which imply a **VALUE** behind them (who's to say that value is "wrong"?) and may cause behaviours no-one can accept as **RATIONAL**. Secular and religious philosophers argue for an **OBJECTIVE** basis coming from **REASON** (Kant, Pope Benedict) or **EXPERIENCE** (for example, the **UTILITARIAN** argument that some actions cause PAIN and misery and so are **EVIL**).

## KEY QUOTES - RELATIVISM

1. *"There are no absolute universal moral standards binding on all men at all times". John Ladd*

2. *"Values are merely culturally approved habits". Ruth Benedict*

3. *"The very eyes with which we see the problem are conditioned by the long traditional habits of our own society". Ruth Benedict*

4. *"Normative relativism puts forward a normative principle: what is right or good for one individual or society is not right or good for another, even if the situations involved are similar..which seems to violate the principles of consistency and universalization". William Frankena*

5. *"There is no objective truth". J.L.Mackie*

6. *"We are in danger of falling into a tyranny of relativism". Pope Benedict*

7. *"The recognition of moral relativity can make a positive*

*contribution to the resolution of an important human problem – the recognition of equal human worth". David Wong*

8. *"The fact that moral principles are weakly dependent doesn't show that ethical relativism is valid. In spite of this weak dependency on non-moral factors, there could still be a set of general moral norms applicable to all cultures and even recognised in most, which a culture could disregard at its own expense". Louis Pojman*

## CONFUSIONS TO AVOID - RELATIVISM

1. "Relativism means anything goes" – this isn't true. Relativism implies we give reasons for our moral viewpoints and that we have views of right and wrong, it's just that there is no overarching principle I can appeal to to arbitrate between my moral view and yours. Even my way of reasoning is culturally conditioned - so the faith in pure reason that Kant had doesn't work either.

2. "Cultural relativism is the same as normative relativism" – this isn't the case. Cultural relativism is describing how different cultures have different moral viewpoints, whereas normative relativism goes a step further and argues that all values are inevitably culturally captive and there can never be an objective truth. This is a step James Rachels argues is invalid.

# Natural Law

A normative **DEONTOLOGICAL** theory coming from a **TELEOLOGICAL** worldview as Aristotle argues that the good is defined by the **RATIONAL ENDS** or **FINAL CAUSES** which people by **NATURE** pursue. "Natural Law is the sharing in the eternal law by intelligent creatures" argues **AQUINAS** and calls these rational ends **OBJECTS OF THE WILL**. Key **ASSUMPTIONS** are that we have a fixed human nature, there is an eternal law in God himself, and the **SYNDERESIS** principle – that we naturally "do good and avoid evil".

## KEY TERMS

- **NATURAL LAW** - "right reason in agreement with nature". Cicero

- **SYNDERSIS** - the assumption that we by nature seek to do good and avoid evil – or have an innate knowledge of first principles (the primary precepts).

- **PRIMARY PRECEPTS** - principles known innately which define the rational ends or goods of human existence.

- **SECONDARY PRECEPTS** - applications of the primary precepts using human reason, which are not absolute.

- **APPARENT GOODS** - acts done from reason which do not correspond to the natural law.

- **REAL GOODS** - acts done from human reason which

correspond to the natural law.

- **NATURAL RIGHTS** - rights given to human beings because of their very nature as human.

- **ETERNAL LAW** - the law as conceived by God.

- **DIVINE LAW** - the law revealed to humankind in the Bible.

- **HUMAN LAW** - the laws we establish by human reason as our social laws.

*Synderesis:* 'each precious child, born with the desire to do good, and avoid evil'

# AQUINAS' ARGUMENT

**AQUINAS** sought to reconcile Christian thought with Greek thinking (**ARISTOTLE**'s works) discovered in Islamic libraries at the **FALL OF TOLEDO** (1085), when Christian armies reconquered Spain. He sees goodness in the **DIVINE ESSENCE** (nature of God) which has a purpose – the **ETERNAL LAW** – reflected in our **HUMAN NATURE** and the ends we rationally pursue. A key assumption Aquinas makes is called the **SYNDERESIS** principle, that we naturally "do good and avoid evil" – which is the opposite of the **REFORMATION** assumption that "all have sinned and fall short of God's glory" (Romans 3:23). We are born with good natures, able to reason and so pursue good ends or objects of the will. The **DIVINE LAW** reflects God's eternal law and is revealed in holy **SCRIPTURE** (eg Ten Commandments of Exodus 20). From these observable rational ends we get the **PRIMARY PRECEPTS**.

## PRIMARY PRECEPTS

There are five observable "goods" or rational ends we pursue. (Acronym **POWER**).

- **P**reservation of life

- **O**rdered society

- **W**orship of God

- **E**ducation

- **R**eproduction

These reflect the **DIVINE WILL** because God designed us with a rational nature in His image. Notice that **VERITATIS SPLENDOR** (1995 Papal document) has subtly changed these – Worship of God becomes **APPRECIATION OF BEAUTY** (to fit with our agnostic age), and it adds **CONCERN** for the **ENVIRONMENT** to reflect the new emphasis on stewardship rather than **DOMINION** (Genesis 1:24 "and let man have dominion over the earth"). This indicates that **NATURAL LAW** is not as **ABSOLUTE** as we sometimes think. The fourth type of law is **HUMAN LAW**. For society to **FLOURISH** (Greek telos of **EUDAIMONIA** sees happiness as personal and social flourishing) we need to bring our law in line with the **ETERNAL LAW** of God, or put another way, make it appropriate for **RATIONAL** human beings to fulfil their Godly destiny – being with God forever and being Christlike.

## SECONDARY PRECEPTS

These are **APPLICATIONS** of the **PRIMARY PRECEPTS** and may change eg as our society changes, science advances our understanding of the Divine Mind, or a situation demands it (eg Thou shalt not kill gets suspended in times of war). Aquinas suggests **POLYGAMY** (many wives) may sometimes be justified. We don't necessarily have to accept **ROMAN CATHOLIC** applications eg Abortion is tantamount to murder, Euthanasia breaks the **SANCTITY OF LIFE**, Contraception goes against the natural purpose of sex, which is **REPRODUCTION**, and homosexual behaviour is **INTRINSICALLY DISORDERED** (the phrase used in **HUMANAE VITAE**, 1967). There is another assumption here that there is **ONE HUMAN NATURE** – heterosexual-and so there can't be a gay nature. Modern Psychology (eg **JUNG**) suggests we have male and female aspects to our natures and **CHINESE** philosophy has always talked in terms of **YING** and **YANG** – the two aspects of our nature.

# APPARENT GOODS

We cannot consciously sin because our nature is such that we believe we are "doing good and avoiding evil" – the **SYNDERESIS PRINCIPLE** - even when practising genocide. However, though we rationalise it, this clearly breaks the **ETERNAL LAW** reflected in the **NATURAL LAW** that most rational humans want to **PRESERVE LIFE** (primary precept **P** of **POWER** acronym above). We cannot flourish if we break the Natural Law – in this sense we are being sub-human and irrational (even though we believe otherwise). **AQUINAS** calls these **APPARENT GOODS** - which we mistakenly believe (eg Hitler's genocide) are **REAL GOODS**. We can sin, but not consciously, which is why **EVANGELICALS** dislike Natural law theory – arguing it is unrealistic (our very **REASON** is distorted by sin) and unbiblical (it seems to deny Paul's teaching on **ORIGINAL SIN**, inherited from **ADAM** after the **FALL**).

# STRENGTHS

**AUTONOMOUS AND RATIONAL:** Natural law is an autonomous, rational theory and it is wrong to say that you have to believe in God to make sense of it. Aquinas speaks of "the pattern of life lived according to reason". You could be a Darwinian atheist and believe in natural law derived by empirical observation, with the primary precept of survival (Aquinas' preservation of life). Richard **DAWKINS** (The Selfish Gene) goes so far as to argue for a natural genetic tendency to be altruistic: a lust to be nice. "The theory of Natural Law suggests..morality is **AUTONOMOUS**. It has its own questions, its own methods of answering them, and its own standards of truth, and religious considerations are not the point". Rachels (2006:56)

**AN EXALTED VIEW OF HUMAN BEINGS:** We use reason to work

out how to live. So we are not slaves to our passions or our genes. Natural Law has a purpose: a flourishing society and a person fulfilled and happy - **EUDAIMONIA**. It is not ultimately about restricting us by rules, but setting us free to fulfil our proper purpose or **TELOS**, inherent in our design: to rationally assent to personal growth. If we can agree on our purpose we can agree on what morality is for. Moreover, we don't have to accept the fact/value division inherent in Moore or Ayer's philosophy. "The natural world is not to be regarded merely as a realm of facts, devoid of value or purpose. Instead, the world is conceived to be a **RATIONAL ORDER** with value and purpose built into its very nature". Rachels (2006: 50)

**FLEXIBLE:** Natural Law is not inflexible. The primary precepts may be general and unchanging, but as Aquinas argued, **SECONDARY PRECEPTS** can change depending on circumstances, culture and worldview. The Doctrine of **DOUBLE EFFECT** is also a way to escape the moral dilemmas which exist when two rules conflict, (See Louis Pojman 2006: 47-51) – so not as **ABSOLUTE** as textbooks suggest.

## WEAKNESSES

**A FIXED HUMAN NATURE:** Aquinas believes in one fixed, shared human nature with certain natural properties eg heterosexual. But evidence suggests there are gay genes and so there is no one natural human nature, but many. This is actually a form of the **NATURALISTIC FALLACY**, the movement from an "is" to an "ought". "It may be that sex does produce babies, but it does not follow that sex ought or ought not to be engaged in only for that purpose. Facts are one thing, values are another". Rachels (2006:52)

**AN OPTIMISTIC VIEW:** Aquinas believes that we possess **INNATELY** (are born with) a "tendency to do good and avoid evil", the

**SYNDERESIS** principle. This is in contrast with Augustine who believes that, due to the Fall, we are born into sin, the sin of Adam, or perhaps the view of psychologists like Freud, that natural selfishness becomes moralised by upbringing and socialisation.

**IMMORAL OUTCOMES:** Natural Law has been interpreted to ban contraception, because this interferes with the natural primary precept of reproduction. But, a. it's not clear that sex is exclusively for reproduction, in fact, the function of human bonding may be primary, and b. the consequence of this policy in Africa has had evil effects of the spread of **AIDS** and the birth of **AIDS** infected children who often become orphans living on the streets.

## KEY QUOTES - NATURAL LAW

1.  *"The Natural Law is the sharing in the eternal law by intelligent creatures" . Thomas Aquinas*

2.  *"Our ultimate end is unrelated good, namely God, who alone can fill our will to the brim because of infinite goodness". Thomas Aquinas*

3.  *"The Natural Law is unchangeable in its first principles, but in its secondary principles it may be changed through some special causes hindering the following of the primary precepts". Thomas Aquinas*

4.  *"The Natural Law involves universality as it is inscribed in the rational nature of a person; it makes itself felt in every person endowed with reason". Veritatis Splendor (1995)*

5.	*"There exist acts which are always seriously wrong by reason of their object". Veritatis Splendor (1995)*

6.	*"Every marital act must of necessity retain its intrinsic relationship to the procreation of human life". Humanae Vitae (1967)*

7.	*"The theory of Natural law suggests morality is autonomous. It has its own questions, its own methods of answering them and its own standards of truth. Religious considerations are not the point". James Rachels*

8.	*"The world is conceived as a rational order with value and purpose built into its very nature". James Rachels*

## CONFUSIONS - NATURAL LAW

1. "Natural" means "as we see in the natural world". This isn't true because many things we see in the natural world we would argue are immoral (eg killing the weak which animals do all the time). "Natural" means something closer to "appropriate for our rational human nature", for example, we may naturally feel lust but it is irrational and wrong to seek to indulge this lust with a complete stranger.

2. "Natural law is dogmatic and inflexible". This is a wrong reading of Aquinas who himself argues that the **SECONDARY PRECEPTS** are liable to change with circumstances and our developed understanding. It is quite possible to be a natural law theorist and argue in favour of contraception on the grounds that it is necessary to save lives and reduce population growth.

# Kantian Ethics

A **NORMATIVE** theory (tells you what is right and wrong/what you ought to do), that is **DEONTOLOGICAL** (acts are intrinsically right and wrong in themselves, stressing rules and duties), **ABSOLUTIST** (applies universally in all times, places, situations) and is **A PRIORI** (derived from reason alone, not experience).

## AUTONOMY

The key Kantian assumption is that we are **AUTONOMOUS** moral agents (self-ruled) which have free choice and free reason, rather than **HETERONOMOUS** meaning "ruled by others", where the others could be God, your peer group, or the Church. Kant adopted the **ENLIGHTENMENT** slogan "dare to reason" and was awakened out of his slumbers by reading Jean-Jacques **ROUSSEAU**'s theory of the social contract.

## GOOD WILL

Kant argues that the only thing that is morally good without exception is the **GOOD WILL**. A person of good will is someone motivated by **DUTY** alone. They are not motivated by self-interest, happiness or a feeling of sympathy. The good will is an **INTRINSIC** good (it is good in itself and not as a means to something else) and it doesn't matter if it doesn't bring about good consequences. Even if the good will achieved nothing good – even if it were combined with all manner of other evils – "it would shine forth like a jewel, having full value in itself". He contrasts this with other qualities (such as courage) which **CAN** be good but might also be bad depending on the situation (eg a courageous suicide bomber) which are **EXTRINSIC** goods as they depend on the circumstances.

## DUTY

Kant argues that we must follow our duty. It is not about what we want to do (our **INCLINATIONS**) or what will lead to the best consequences: only the action which springs from duty is a moral action. Doing your duty (for example, helping a beggar) may be pleasurable, but this cannot be the reason why you did your duty (the **MOTIVE**). For it to be moral you have to act because it is your duty, and **FOR NO OTHER REASON**.

## CATEGORICAL IMPERATIVE (C.I.)

How do you know what your duty is? Kant argues that this comes from the **CATEGORICAL IMPERATIVE**. It is categorical because it applies to us universally – simply because we have rational wills. By contrast a **HYPOTHETICAL IMPERATIVE** takes the form "If you want X, then you must do Y" (for example, if you want to lose weight, then you must stop eating so much). The difference is the categorical imperative applies to us unconditionally, without any reference to a goal we might have (it is simply the form "You must do Y").

### C.I. 1 THE FORMULA OF LAW

*"So act that the maxim of your action may be willed as a universal law for all humanity".*

For any action to be moral, you must be able to **CONSISTENTLY UNIVERSALISE** it. For example, if you decide not to keep a promise, then you must be able to consistently imagine a world where

**EVERYONE** doesn't keep their promises – something Kant thought was impossible (because then no-one would believe a promise and so promise-keeping would vanish). He calls this a **CONTRADICTION IN NATURE** because the very nature of the thing – promising – is destroyed and so the action becomes self-contradictory.

### C.I. 2 FORMULA OF ENDS

*"Never treat people simply as a means to an end but always also as an end in themselves".*

People are **RATIONAL** and **AUTONOMOUS** (self-legislators) and so are worthy of respect. We cannot ONLY use them as a means for getting something else, but always as rational beings with dignity. We universalise our common humanity – which means we treat others as equals, with rights.

### C.I.3 FORMULA OF AUTONOMY

Kant imagines a community of purely rational agents, each of whom is a **LEGISLATOR** (someone who decides laws) and a **SUBJECT** (someone who has to follow those laws) in what he calls a **KINGDOM OF ENDS**. We can only act on moral laws that would be accepted by this fully rational community – we belong to a moral parliament where we are free participators in the law-making process. This introduces an important **SOCIAL** aspect to Kantian ethics. "Kantian ethics is the ethics of democracy", argues James Rachels.

## SUMMUM BONUM

The **SUMMUM BONUM** or "supreme good" is **VIRTUE** (a person of 'good will' who follows their duty by applying the Categorical

Imperative) combined with **HAPPINESS**. We should not act in order to get happiness (because moral action should only involve doing our duty for duty's sake), but the ideal is that we should be happy to the degree that we **DESERVE** to be happy. This is obviously not something that can be found in this life – we see bad people living happy lives and good people living unhappy lives – therefore the Summum Bonum must be able to be achieved in the **AFTERLIFE**.

## THREE POSTULATES

Kant argued there are three necessary postulates (or propositions) for morality:

1. **FREEDOM** (we must be free to make moral decisions).

2. **IMMORTALITY** (there must be an afterlife in order to achieve the summum bonum).

3. **GOD** (necessary to guarantee the moral law and to judge fairly and reward or punish).

## STRENGTHS OF KANT

It's **REASONABLE** – pretty much what most people consider morality to be about (such as universalising your behaviour). The various formulations of the Categorical Imperative take the **DIGNITY** and **EQUALITY** of human beings very seriously. The **INNOCENT** are protected by the universal equality given to all human beings.

## WEAKNESSES

It is **INFLEXIBLE** as absolutes have to be applied in all situations irrespective of what we consider to be the wisest choice. For example, Kant considers the case of a crazy axeman who arrives at a house where a friend is hiding and asks "is your friend in there?" because truth-telling is an **ABSOLUTE** we are supposed to say "yes". Kant also seems to make a clear distinction between our **EMOTIONS** and the ethical choice done from duty alone - but is it really morally doubtful if I act out of emotion like compassion and not just from **DUTY** alone? Also, what happens when two duties **CONFLICT** (for example, the duty to preserve my friend's life conflicts with my duty to tell the truth - Kant's own example where he insists we tell the truth whatever happens). Surely **CONSEQUENCES** do matter?  Can we not have a **HIERARCHY OF DUTIES** as **W.D.ROSS** argues so that preserving life is ranked higher than truth-telling?

# KEY QUOTES - KANT

1.  *"It is impossible to conceive of anything in the world good without qualification except the good will".* Kant

2.  *"Kant places the stern voice of duty at the heart of the moral life".* Robert Arrington

3.  *"The highest created good is a world where rational beings are happy and worthy of happiness".* Kant

4.  *"With sufficient ingenuity almost every precept can be consistently universalised".* Alasdair MacIntyre

5.  *"There is more to the moral point of view than being willing to universalise one's rules".* William Frankena

# CONFUSIONS - KANT

1. "Duty means blind obedience". This is what Adolf Eichmann implied in his trial in 1962 - but it's not Kant's view of duty which involves reasoning through the **UNIVERSALISABILITY** of your action and treating all human beings with equal respect.

2. "Duty means ignoring emotion". This is a possible reading of Kant, but not the only one. Another reading is to say that Kant saw duty as the primary motive and so long as emotions don't conflict with duty then having moral emotions is fine - just don't base your reason on emotion.

# Bentham's Act Utilitarianism

**BENTHAM** (1748-1832) was a social reformer who believed that the law should serve human needs and welfare. Where **JUSTICE** was **RETRIBUTIVE** he wanted to see it **REFORMING** and acting as a **DETERRENCE** – there had to be a real social benefit outweighing the pain to the criminal, and with a better **DISTRIBUTION** of resources, but all in the cause of the **GREATEST HAPPINESS PRINCIPLE (GHP)** – the motive was to reduce suffering and increase happiness for everyone. The theory is **TELEOLOGICAL** because it measures likely consequences of **ACTIONS**, and **HEDONIC** because Bentham believed pleasure (Greek: hedon) was the key motive and could be quantified. So there is an **EMPIRICAL**, objective measure of goodness.

## MOTIVATION

There is one **MORAL** good – pleasure, and one evil – pain. "Nature has placed mankind under two **SOVEREIGN** masters, pain and pleasure". Right actions are on balance pleasurable, wrong actions are on balance painful. Bentham's is therefore a theory of **PSYCHOLOGICAL HEDONISM** (Hedonism - pleasure-seeking).

## HEDONIC CALCULUS

The **HEDONIC CALCULUS** is a way of measuring pleasure and pain, so the consequences of an act can be assessed as a score in units of happiness called **HEDONS** (plus for pleasure, minus for pain). The seven criteria are (acronym **PRRICED**): **P**urity, **R**ichness, **R**eliability, **I**ntensity, **C**ertainty, **E**xtent, **D**uration. In this assessment "everyone is to count as one and no-one as more than one" (Bentham), so there is strict **EQUALITY**.

## QUANTITATIVE PLEASURE

Bentham believed "pushpin is as good as poetry" (pushpin – a pub game = playing a slot machine in today's terms). Pleasure is purely **QUANTITATIVE** so we can't award more hedons to listening to Mozart or painting a picture or grasping philosophy. Mill, who was saved from mental breakdown by **WORDSWORTH**'s poetry, really objected to this. According to Bentham, we can compare a small child's delight in a new toy with someone else's delight in a new girlfriend. A **PIG** enjoying a good wallow is of more value than **SOCRATES** having a sightly sad think. Hence "the pig philosophy".

## PLEASURE MACHINES

**JCC SMART** (1973:18-21) asks us to imagine a pleasure machine where we can be wired up every day and passively enjoy every pleasure imaginable (note - addiction often operates like this as a kind of refuge in a supposed pleasure - like drink). **ALDOUS HUXLEY** wrote of a brave new world where people popped **SOMA** tablets to make them happy (there were 41m antidepressant prescriptions last year in the UK). Bentham can have no problems with this, but **MILL** saw happiness as a wider idea involving **ACTIVITY**, and realistic goals and expectations (closer to what my therapist might advise or what **ARISTOTLE** argues).

purity

remote -ness

reprod- ucability

intensity

certainty

extent

duration

HEDON-O-METER

JERRY BENTHAM'S 12 FRUIT SLURPER

## STRENGTHS - BENTHAM

There is a **SIMPLICITY** in Bentham's calculation, and a radical **EQUALITY**. The **TELOS** of increasing human welfare is attractive and **COMMON SENSE**. His ideas drove **SOCIAL REFORM** – and he designed a more humane prison called a **PANOPTICON** – never built in the UK, but in Barcelona. There is a lack of snobbery in his classification of all pleasures as **EQUALLY VALID** – why should Mozart be thought better than Rap music (at least in giving pleasure)?

## WEAKNESSES

Bentham focuses only on **ACTIONS** so we have to keep on calculating (he doesn't allow us to have **RULES** to make life easier). He equates **PLEASURE** with **HAPPINESS** – but they don't seem to be equivalent (ask the athlete training for the Olympics whether the toil is pleasurable – but it doesn't mean a lack of contentment with training). We can always ask "you're going to the nightclub, but is that a **GOOD** idea?" ("Good" meaning "promoting your welfare"). Bentham implies pleasure is **MEASURABLE** (it isn't - how can we compare my hedon with yours?). Finally, he has no answer for Smart's **PLEASURE MACHINE** or Huxley's **SOMA** tablet (of course, they were writing two centuries later so even if his stuffed skeleton, residing in a cupboard in London University, could talk, we don't know what it would say!).

# KEY QUOTES - BENTHAM

1.  *"Nature has placed mankind under two sovereign masters, pain and pleasure. It is for them to point out what we ought to do as well as determine what we should do". Jeremy Bentham*

2.  *"In every human breast, self-regarding interest is predominant over social interest; each person's own individual interest over the interests of all other persons taken together". Jeremy Bentham, Book of Fallacies, p 392*

3.  *"The community is a fictitious body", and it is but "the sum of the interests of the several members who compose it". Jeremy Bentham*

4.  *"Prejudice apart, the game of pushpin is of equal value with the arts and sciences of music and poetry. If the game of pushpin furnishes more pleasure, it is more valuable than either". Jeremy Bentham*

# Mill's Rule Utilitarianism

The weak **RULE UTILITARIANISM** (RU) of John Stuart Mill (1806-73) is a **TELEOLOGICA**L (telos = goal) theory based on a definition of goodness as the **BALANCE** of happiness over misery. This is a measurable, **EMPIRICAL** idea – measure the happiness effects of likely consequences – giving an **OBJECTIVE** measure of goodness. Mill was against the **INTUITIONISTS** which he found too **SUBJECTIVE**. Mill argues that happiness is most likely to be maximised by generally following a set of **RULES** which society has found, by experience, maximise utility. But the rules can develop and in cases of moral dilemmas, we should revert to being **ACT UTILITARIANS** (AU), so weak **RU** because the rules aren't absolute, but are **GUIDELINES**.

## MILL v BENTHAM

Mill disliked three aspects of **BENTHAM**'s version.

The swinish implications of categorising all pleasures as of equal value – drinking beer v. listening to Mozart.

The emphasis on pleasure alone, as Mill was influenced by **ARISTOTLE**'s views on virtue (eg the importance of **SYMPATHY** for others).

The problem of **JUSTICE** and **RIGHTS** – how do we prevent one innocent person or group being sacrificed for the general happiness of the majority? So Mill devotes the last chapter of his essay to **JUSTICE**.

## MILL ON HAPPINESS

Mill's definition of a happy life has three elements – pleasure (varied and rich) and absence of pain, **AUTONOMY** (the free choice of a life goal), and **ACTIVITY** (motivated by virtues like sympathy eg Mill used to hand out leaflets advising about contraception and campaigned for women's rights).

"**HAPPINESS** is not a life of rapture, but moments of such, in an existence with few and transitory pains, many and various pleasures, with a decided predominance of the **ACTIVE** over the passive, and having as a foundation of the whole, not to expect more from life than it is capable of bestowing". JS Mill

## HIGHER AND LOWER PLEASURES

Mill was saved from a nervous breakdown in his 20s by the **ROMANTIC MOVEMENT** eg Wordsworth's Lyrical Ballads. To him poetry was infinitely superior to **PUSHPIN** (a pub game). So "better to be Socrates dissatisfied than a fool satisfied". The **LOWER** bodily pleasures (food, sex, drink, football) were of les value than the HIGHER pleasures (reading, thinking, listening to Mozart). So Mill followed **ARISTOTLE** in seeing education as of vital importance (the supreme Greek value is **CONTEMPLATION** to gain wisdom). Only a person who'd experienced both could really judge the difference in **QUALITY** (so we say qualitative pleasure is superior to quantitative). He called those who hadn't experienced both "inferior beings". Does this make Mill a snob?

# RULES

Mill has been called an "inconsistent utilitarian" (Alasdair MacIntyre) – because as his essay goes on he moves from **ACT** to **RULE** utilitarianism. We use generations of **PAST EXPERIENCE** to form rules, so we don't have to do a calculation to know whether **MURDER** or **THEFT** is "right". We inherit **BELIEFS** "and the beliefs which have thus come down are the **RULES** of morality for the multitude" (JS Mill). These are not fixed but "admit of continual improvement" – so not **ABSOLUTE**. The **FIRST PRINCIPLE** is utility (or the Greatest Happiness Principle) and then **SECONDARY PRINCIPLES** (rules) come from this and are constantly evaluated against the first principle. Just as navigation is based on astronomy doesn't mean the sailor goes back to the stars every time – no, Mill reminds us, he uses an **ALMANAC** – so, argues Mill, human beings follow a code book of rules passed down from previous generations as the best way to be happy.

# JUSTICE

Bernard **WILLIAMS** argued that Utilitarianism violates our **MORAL INTEGRITY** by encouraging us to do things we would find repulsive – like his example of Jim who is invited to kill one Indian as an honoured guest in order to save nineteen others. This is the problem of **INJUSTICE** – the Southern States may have enjoyed lynching innocent people in the 1920s but this doesn't make it right. Mill argues that unhappiness is caused by selfishness, by people "acting only for themselves", and that for a person to be happy they need "to cultivate a fellow feeling with the collective interests of mankind" and "in the **GOLDEN RULE** of Jesus we find the whole ethics of utility" (JS Mill). So we need to defend personal **RIGHTS** and "Justice is a name for certain moral requirements, which, regarded collectively, stand higher in the scale of **SOCIAL UTILITY**, and are therefore of more paramount obligation, than any others", and "justice is a name for certain classes of **MORAL RULES**, which concern the essentials of human **WELL-BEING**". Rights, justice and the virtue of sympathy stop selfish self-interest destroying the happiness of others. So we escape the problem of Jim and the Indians as we would never shoot one indian (violate their right to life) to save nineteen.

## ACT OR RULE?

**LOUIS POJMAN** argues (2006:111) that we can adopt a **MULTILEVEL** approach (this is what Mill seems to be doing in talking about **PRIMARY** and **SECONDARY** principles). So we can have three levels if we wish: rules of thumb to live by which generally maximise utility, a second set of rules for resolving conflicts between these, and a third process – an **ACT** utilitarian one, for assessing a difficult situation according to the **GREATEST HAPPINESS PRINCIPLE** or GHP (eg lying to save a friend). But in this way philosophers like **J.O.URMSON** argue that **RULE** utilitarianism collapses into **ACT** utilitarianism. Mill might counter that we don't have the time, the wisdom, or the resources to keep calculating every action and this multilevel approach is therefore realistic and practical in a way that **KANT**'s deontology is unrealistic and impractical because it cannot handle **MORAL DILEMMAS**.

## STRENGTHS

**RATIONALITY** and **PRACTICALITY**.    Utilitarian ethics rests on a rational calculation of numbers of people whose pleasure or happiness is maximised. There is a clarity and simplicity to this. **EQUALITY** is central. Bentham wrote "everyone is to count as one, and no-one as more than one". This radical idea implies that everyone has equal weight in the utility calculation. **MILL** adds equal **RIGHTS**. Suppose, on an equal vote, you all vote for my dismissal (or even death) in line with maximising general happiness? "The utilitarian emphasis on impartiality must be a part of any defensible moral theory". (Rachels, 2006:114). Finally, utilitarianism takes account of the **FUTURE** – issues of climate change, potential future wars and famines all suggest we need an ethical theory that takes into account those yet unborn.

## WEAKNESSES

**MOTIVE**, "why should I maximise pleasure or happiness?" We can't agree how to define pleasure or happiness". Bentham and Mill don't notice the difficulty of the concept of "pleasure" a fatal objection at the outset", Anscombe (1958:2). Then there is a difficulty in making me think of the interests (happiness) of others. Mill tries to bring "sympathy" in as a kind of virtue or psychological motive. **DISTRIBUTION** problems emerge when I try to maximise **TOTAL** not **AVERAGE** happiness – for example, low tax for the rich may raise the total but reduce average happiness, because the 10% super rich are much, much happier. Finally **CONSEQUENCES** are hard to calculate if you don't have the omniscience of God. The **IRAQ WAR** may have seemed justifiable by the Greatest Happiness Principle - but looking with hindsight we might argue - better a Saddam Hussein in power than a million deaths?

# KEY QUOTES - MILL'S UTILITARIANISM

1. *"It is better to be a human being dissatisfied than a pig satisfied; better Socrates dissatisfied than a fool satisfied". J.S.Mill*

2. *"Happiness is...moments of rapture...in an existence of few and transitory pains, many and various pleasures, with a predominance of the active over the passive...not to expect more from life than it is capable of bestowing". J.S. Mill*

3. *"Whatever we adopt as the fundamental principle of Morality, we require subordinate principles to apply it by". (Fundamental principle = happiness is good, subordinate principles = rules) J.S. Mill*

4. *"By the improvement of education, the feeling of unity with our fellow-creatures shall be as deeply rooted in our character, and to our own consciousness as completely a part of our nature, as the horror of crime is in an ordinarily well brought up young person". (= sympathy) JS Mill*

5. *"To have a right, then, is, I conceive, to have something which society should defend me in possession of. If the objector asks why? I can give no other answer than general utility". J.S.Mill*

6. *"Justice is a name for certain moral requirements, which, regarded collectively, stand higher in the scale of social utility, and are therefore of more paramount obligation, than any others: though particular cases may occur in which some other social duty is so important as to overrule any one of the general*

*maxims of justice. Thus to save a life it may not only be allowable, but a duty, to steal, or take by force, the necessary food or medicine, or to kidnap, or compel to officiate, the only qualified medical practitioner". J.S.Mill (note - so RU collapses into AU)*

7.  *"I account the justice which is grounded on utility to be the chief part, and incomparably the most sacred and binding part, of all morality. Justice is a name for certain classes of moral rules, which concern the essentials of human well-being more nearly, and are therefore of more absolute obligation, than any other rules for the guidance of life". J.S.Mill*

8.  *BERNARD WILLIAMS argues that "because our relation to the world is partly given by moral feelings, and by a sense of what we can or cannot "live with", to regard those feelings....as happening outside one's moral self is to lose one's moral identity; to lose, in the most literal way, one's integrity". (Utilitarianism For and Against page 104)*

# CONFUSIONS - MILL

1. Was Mill an Act or Rule Utilitarian? He is sometimes described as a **WEAK RULE UTILITARIAN**. Mill believed that generally we should follow the rule as this reflects society's view of what maximises happiness from past social experience. But when a pressing utilitarian need arises we should break the rule and so become an act utilitarian.

2. "Mill took Bentham's view that happiness equates to pleasure". Sometimes Mill seems to argue this, but it's truer to say Mill's view is close to **ARISTOTLE**'s that happiness means "personal and social flourishing". So to Mill the individual cannot be happy without the guarantee of certain rules and rights and clear goals to aim for.

# Situation Ethics - Christian Relativism

Situation Ethics is a **NORMATIVE** theory (tells you what is right/wrong – what you ought to do), that is **TELEOLOGICAL** and **CONSEQUENTIALIST** (acts are right or wrong if they bring about good/bad consequences, or can be seen as instrumentally good/bad) and **RELATIVIST** (there are no universal rules as actions depend on circumstances; there is just one general universal value – that of agape love). It is also **CHRISTIAN**, based on the principle of sacrificial love (**AGAPE**).

## INTRODUCTION

Joseph Fletcher (1966) argued there are three approaches to ethics:

1. **LEGALISTIC** – someone who follows absolute rules and laws. Fletcher rejects this as it leads to **UNTHINKING OBEDIENCE** and needs elaborate systems of exceptions and compromises.

2. **ANTINOMIAN** – (nomos is Greek for law, so anti-law) or someone who rejects all rules and laws (Fletcher rejects this as it would lead to social **CHAOS**).

3. **SITUATIONAL** – Fletcher argues that each individual situation is different and absolute rules are too demanding and restrictive. Instead we should decide what is the most **LOVING** course of action (**AGAPE**). The Situationist has respect for laws and tradition, but they are only guidelines to how to achieve this

loving outcome, and thus they may be broken if the other course of action would result in more love.

However, Situation Ethics is not **FULLY** relativist: it has an absolute principle (love) that is non-negotiable.

## FOUR WORKING PRINCIPLES

In Situation Ethics there are **FOUR WORKING PRINCIPLES** (Fletcher's own term)

1. **PRAGMATISM** – (what you propose must be practical – work in practice).

2. **RELATIVISM** – (there are no fixed, absolute rules – all decisions are relative to **AGAPE** love. If love demands that you steal food, then you should steal food.

3. **POSITIVISM** – (Kant and Natural Law are based on reason as both theories argue reason can uncover the right course of action). Fletcher disagrees with this: you have to start with a **POSITIVE** choice or commitment – you need to want to do good. There is no rational answer to the question "why should I love?"

4. **PERSONALISM** – (people come first: you cannot sacrifice people to rules or laws)

# SIX FUNDAMENTAL PRINCIPLES

1. Nothing is good in itself except **LOVE** (it is the only thing that is absolutely good, the only thing with intrinsic value).

2. Jesus replaced the law with love or **AGAPE** ("The ruling norm of Christian decision is love, nothing else". Joseph Fletcher).

3. Love and **JUSTICE** are the same thing (if love is put into practice it can only result in fair treatment and fair distribution).

4. Love desires the good of **OTHERS** (it does not have favourites, but this doesn't mean we have to LIKE them).

5. Only the **END JUSTIFIES THE MEANS** (if an action causes harm, it is wrong. If good comes of it, it is right).

6. Love's decisions are made in each **SITUATION**.

## STRENGTHS OF SITUATION ETHICS

It takes **INDIVIDUALS** and their needs seriously. It's also **FLEXIBLE** and also allows us to make judgements in situations where two moral principles **CONFLICT**. **LOVE** is an important value somewhat neglected by other theories as the sympathy of Mill's utilitarian ethics is not quite as strong as the **AGAPE** of Joseph Fletcher.

## WEAKNESSES OF SITUATION ETHICS

**LOVE** is a very demanding value to place at the centre of your ethics - can anyone love sacrificially all the time? Mustn't we be selfish some of the time? Like all **CONSEQUENTIALIST** theories it's impossible to calculate into the future making this particular love calculation **IMPOSSIBLE**. William Barclay argues that Fletcher fails to realise the value of law - as an expression fo the collective wisdom of generations before us, so the moral law is a guide which we shouldn't throw away so easily. Law also defines the **FABRIC** of society.

## KEY QUOTES - SITUATION ETHICS

1.   *"Love alone is always good and right in every situation". Joseph Fletcher (1966:69)*

2.   *"There can be and often is a conflict between law and love". Joseph Fletcher (1966:70)*

3.   *"Too much law means the obliteration of the individual; too much individualism means a weakening of the law...there is a place for law as the encourager of morality". William Barclay*

4.   *"Love is the ultimate law because it is the negation of law; it is absolute because it concerns everything concrete". Paul Tillich*

5.   *In 1952 POPE PIUS XII called situation ethics "an individualistic and subjective appeal to the concrete circumstances of actions to justify decisions in opposition to the NATURAL LAW or God's revealed will'.*

# CONFUSIONS - SITUATION ETHICS

1. "Situation ethics is Christian relativism".   This idea needs careful handling.  In fact there is one non-negotiable absolute at the heart of Situation Ethics - agape love.  But this is a principle, not a rule. Therefore as it is applied, it is made relative to the most loving outcome.  Fletcher himself describes Situation ethics as "relativistic" as it "relativises the absolute, it does not absolutise the relative". Compare Fletcher with Pastor Dietrich Bonhoeffer who believed the most loving thing was to join the 1944 Stauffenberg bomb plot against Hitler (an action which cost him his life).

2. "Jesus was a situationist".   Again, be careful about a bland statement to this effect.  Jesus maintained he "came not to abolish the law, but to fulfil it", although a key part of his mission seemed to be to overthrow the old Jewish purity code (he didn't like stoning adulterers, see John 8, or treating unclean women as "impure and untouchable", see Mark 5, both required by Leviticus 18-19).  The young man of Mark 7 is commended for keeping the law but then invited to "give up all his possessions and come, follow me!". The nearest Jesus comes to situationism is in the discussion of the parable of the Good Samaritan, where the teacher of the law is invited to "go and do likewise" in each situation requiring agape love (Luke 10:29-37).  Indeed, the parable is worth studying in the light of Fletcher's teaching.  It's about the meaning and application of agape love.

# Divine Command - Christian Absolutism

## SOME DEFINITIONS

Morality depends on God's commands as revealed in Scripture. Sometimes called **THEOLOGICAL VOLUNTARISM,** Divine Command Theories are found in the Franciscan ethics developed by John Duns Scotus (1266-1308), William of Ockham (1285-1347), and Andrew of Neufchateau (1340-1400). Modern evangelicals take a similar view – see the **CHICAGO STATEMENT ON BIBLICAL INERRANCY** (1966) following Bible based reformers Martin Luther (1483-1546) and John Calvin (1509-1564). A modern theorist is Philip Quinn. It is open to the problems of **EUTHYPHRO'S DILEMMA**.

## DEONTOLOGICAL

Something is good because God commands it and wrong because he forbids it – so creates duties (**DEON** = duty in Greek). In the Old Testament God is described as a commander of his people and lays down the law (Exodus 20:1-17). Disobedience is punished by death (eg Moses kills the worshippers of the **GOLDEN CALF**). God's **OMNISCIENT** and **OMNIBENEVOLENT** (all-loving) character underpins the law – gracious, compassionate, merciful, steadfast (Exodus 34:6). In the **NT** Jesus gives a new commandment to love (John 15:7) and says love entails obedience; "if you love me you will obey my commandments". So **AGAPE** is a divine command (if Jesus is God). **AQUINAS** argued that when Abraham went to slay Isaac he did no wrong because "the Lord of life and Death commanded it " (Genesis 22:1-2), and so Abraham would not have been guilty of murder.

## INITIAL PROBLEM

The problem of **ABHORRENT COMMANDS** occurs because, with Abraham and Isaac, God appears to approve of murder, and when the angel of the Lord commands Joshua to kill everyone in the cities of **JERICHO** and **AI**, Joshua is apparently not guilty of genocide (Joshua 8). God is also described as **JEALOUS** (Exodus 34:6-8) and will not tolerate rivals such as **BAAL** the god of the people of Palestine. The 450 prophets of Baal are killed by **ELIJAH** after the challenge – who could rain down fire from heaven? (1 **KINGS** 18:33). Andrew of Neufchateau suggests Abraham would have sinned had he not gone to kill Isaac, even though Isaac was saved by the ram caught in a thicket. In the New Testament Jesus orders the demons to enter a herd of pigs that stampede into the sea (Mark 5), and commands storms to cease and illnesses to be cured: "Be clean!", exclaims Jesus to the Leper.

## EUTHYPHRO

**EUTHYPHRO'S DILEMMA** originates with **PLATO**. Is something good because God commands it, or does God command it because it is good? If goodness = God's commands, there is the **ARBITRARINESS** problem (we need to know God's reasoning too, and if there is no God presumably there is no morality either and "anything goes"), the **EMPTINESS** problem (that the statement becomes an empty **TAUTOLOGY**\* where "God is good" is the same as saying "God is God" which doesn't get us very far) and the **ABHORRENT COMMANDS** problem - that God appears to order genocide in the book of Joshua and practising gays to be stoned in Leviticus. In a

56

**PLURALISTIC** society there are many views of God and what he is saying, and even if we take the Bible as **AUTHORITATIVE** divinely-inspired words, there is still the question – what do those words actually **MEAN**? Language is open-ended and must be understood in context (eg "do not kill" can't be an absolute because Joshua is ordered to slaughter the people of Jericho). So if God's commands are immoral, that makes God immoral – and if goodness comes from elsewhere, that makes God irrelevant to morality – and God himself should be condemned for ordering the **GENOCIDE** of the inhabitants of Jericho and Ai.

## CHARACTER

But Philip Quinn argues "the divine essence constrains the divine will". The essence of God is his essential **CHARACTER** – all-loving, all-knowing and all-powerful. We don't know everything and have to trust God's essential goodness eg in commanding Joshua, because we don't know what would have happened otherwise. So God's command to torture the innocent is conceivable, but impossible given God's character – he would have to be arbitrary and unloving. However on this basis we have to say **JOSHUA** was mistaken because God could not have possibly commanded genocide. Where does this leave the **AUTHORITY** of Scripture and God's supposed commands in Joshua 8?

## SOURCE OF MORALITY

There are only three possible sources of moral value: **DIVINE COMMAND, REASON** and **EXPERIENCE. REASON** implies either **KANT**'s a priori method (universalisability) or Aquinas' a posteriori method (looking at observable goods). Utilitarians argue for **EXPERIENCE** of consequences and their relation to general happiness – an empirical measurement, and **SITUATION ETHICS** argues that there are no rules, only **LOVE** and its relation to consequences. However we must recognise that **REASON** is not a neutral idea – different cultures reason in different ways (eg Buddhist philosophy is very different to Kant's). And if there is to be agreement in a **PLURALISTIC** society this can only come through supplying reasonable grounds for sharing a common value – such as the one Kant gave, "universalise your actions", and indeed Jesus echoes "do to others as you would have them do to you" – the **GOLDEN RULE** (Matthew 7:18). Moreover different cultures handle the **BIBLE** in different ways – **CREATIONISM** is much bigger in the US where court cases are still being fought over **EVOLUTION** v six day creation, and most of us would argue it is not necessary for "women to keep silent in church" (1 Corinthians 11:13) and anyway in Acts 21:9 we read that Philip the evangelist had "four daughters who prophesied", so casting doubts over the view that no women held public leadership. How **ABSOLUTE** is any command?

*A **TAUTOLOGY** is defined as a repetition of the same idea in different words "God's commands are good because God commands them" becomes "God's commands are commanded by God".

# Abortion

## SOME DEFINITIONS

**ABORTION** can be natural (miscarriage) or by medical procedure (using drugs or killing and dismembering a foetus). A **FOETUS** exists from 8 weeks onwards, when the embryo assumes the basic shape of the newborn and all the organs are present; an **EMBRYO** from conception to 8 weeks. **PRE-EMBRYO** is now being used to denote the collection of cells up to 14 days old, before the **PRIMITIVE STREAK** emerges.

## LEGAL POSITION (UK)

The **1967 ABORTION ACT** legalised abortion up to 28 weeks with two doctor's consent a. for medical reasons b. for psychological reasons c. for family reasons d. in cases of disability. The legal term was changed in 1990 to 24 weeks. The age of **VIABILITY** has now dropped to 22 weeks with medical advances. 85% of abortions occur under 18 weeks and there are around 200,000 abortions a year in the UK, representing 25% of pregnancies. Note: we do not have "abortion on demand" in the UK as the consent of two doctors is needed.

## SANCTITY OF LIFE

**SANCTITY OF LIFE** (sacredness) – biblical view **GENESIS 1:27**, we are made in the image of God, and "he knit you together in your mother's womb", **PSALM 139:6**. Human life has **INTRINSIC VALUE** because God himself "became flesh and lived among us" (**JOHN 1:14**). We are not our own, but we belong to God and our life is "on loan" from

God. God appoints the day of our death "the Lord gave and the Lord takes away" **JOB 1:21**. "Do not murder" is a fundamental law, **EXODUS 20:13**, implying respect for all human life, and to the Catholic Church this includes embryonic life.

**SANCTITY OF LIFE** – the Natural Law view. **EVANGELIUM VITAE** (1995 Papal encyclical) argues society has undermined sanctity of life and produced a "culture of death" in its attitude to foetal life, the elderly and the handicapped. So "every person open to truth can recognise the sacred value of human life from its beginning to its end" – as Paul notes "even Gentiles have the law written on their hearts", **ROMANS 2:14-15**. Abortion breaks two **PRIMARY PRECEPTS** of reproduction and preservation of life – as human life begins at conception. We know this through the **SYNDERESIS** principle: innately we "do good and avoid evil" in line with our rational purposes given by our human nature.

**SANCTITY OF LIFE** – weak view. Some prefer the more universal, weaker idea of **RESPECT** for life. As medical science advances we know more eg about disabilities of foetuses or inherited diseases. **SITUATION ETHICS** sees **AGAPE** as a universal good, so the person's situation needs to be paramount, and **STANLEY HAUERWAS** argues that the Church has permitted the taking of life in the past eg when it is in the interests of others, or in cases of martyrdom.

## QUALITY OF LIFE

Peter Singer maintains we would always choose a healthy child over a handicapped one. So "if aborting the abnormal foetus can be followed by having a normal one, it would be wrong not to do this". Note the usual consequentialist problem: how do we know? There is also the question of resources: how much does the handicapped child cost over its life relative to the healthy one? A utilitarian might argue the resources are better spent elsewhere. Is it the most loving outcome (Situation Ethics) to bring a suffering child into the world? Singer employs the **REPLACEMENT** argument – it is always better to replace a less happy child by a happier one – but does this justify **INFANTICIDE** – the killing of less healthy children? Or (as used to happen in Britain in the days of your family doctor) the smothering of abnormal infants?

## HUMAN RIGHTS

Some argue that because the foetus shares the attributes of a person it should have full human rights (including the right to life). The logic of the argument from human rights is given below (P = proposition).

- **P1** - The unborn child is a human life (Is it? Even as a collection of cells?).

- **P2** - It is always wrong to take innocent human life.

- **P3** - Abortion involves the taking of innocent life.

- **P4** - Therefore abortion is wrong.

Notice that the meaning of "human life" has changed from "biological life" to something close to "personhood". The meaning has changed from P1 to P2 – note also the addition of the moral word "innocent".

## WOMEN'S RIGHTS

**JUDITH JARVIS THOMPSON** employs the analogy of the violinist – after his friends kidnap you, you wake up plugged into a sick violinist who needs your kidneys. To unplug the violinist will kill him. It's only for nine months. Do you have the **RIGHT** to unplug the violinist? Does your right to choose what to do with your body outweigh the right to life? (Note the problems with this analogy – for example, pregnant women are not immobile, they are not kidnapped but choose to have sex, the foetus is arguably not actually a person). Thompson argues that to be forced to remain with a dependent being attached to you is **OUTRAGEOUS**.

## PERSONHOOD

**MARY ANNE WARREN** asks "what characteristics make a person?" She lists: consciousness, reason, self-motivated activity, communication, self-awareness. "Genetic humanity is not enough" – we must have at least one of these criteria. "A foetus is a human being which is not yet a person, so cannot have full moral rights", argues Mary Anne Warren. Note: if you apply her criteria this would allow you to kill infants, coma victims and people asleep! **SINGER** agrees with **TOOLEY** who declared a human being "possesses a serious right to life only if it possesses the concept of a self as a continuing **SUBJECT OF EXPERIENCES** and other mental states, and believes that it is itself such a continuing entity". Infants do not qualify. In 1979 **SINGER** wrote, "Human babies are not born self-aware, or capable of grasping that they exist over time. They are not **PERSONS**," therefore, "the life of a newborn is of less value than the life of a pig, a dog, or a chimpanzee".

## WHEN DOES LIFE BEGIN?

**CASTI CONNUBI** (Papal encyclical) – persons at conception. **RC CATECHISM** "from the first moment of his existence a human being must be recognized as having the rights of a person – among which is the inviolable right of every innocent being to life". The **PRIMITIVE STREAK** is the first recognisable feature at 15 days. **QUICKENING**

(movement) occurs at 100 days (c 14 weeks). Some time between 18 and 24 weeks foetus feels pain. **VIABLILTY** (survivability out of the womb) exists around 22 weeks – but probability of survival is low. **MARY ANNE WARREN** sees birth as only morally relevant point as "the extension of equal moral status to foetuses threatens women's most basic rights. Unlike foetuses, women are already persons". **JONATHAN GLOVER** argues it is a matter of degree – a foetus is more of a person than an embryo, a baby is more than a foetus. Ultimately this is a **METAPHYSICAL** question to do with beliefs rather than science. **DON MARQUIS** argued that abortion is wrong because it deprives someone of a future and "the ethics of killing is self-evident" (but how do we know the future? What of the mother's future? How do we weigh mother against child?).

## CHRISTIANS AND ABORTION

There is not one Christian view. The conservative view held by many Catholics and evangelicals holds that life is sacred from the point of conception because God the creator is behind and within this creation (Psalm 139 "God knit you together in your mother's womb"). Catholics follow a **NATURAL LAW** argument, pointing to the **PRIMARY PRECEPT** of preserving innocent life, and the **DIVINE LAW** "do not murder", whereas evangelicals appeal only to **SCRIPTURE**, a Divine Command Theory, eg **PSALM 139:6** "God knit you together in your mother's womb". Liberal Christians might take a **SITUATION ETHICS** view of abortion, arguing that **AGAPE** (sacrificial) love is best maximised by considering the **PERSON** (but which person? mother? child?) and **OUTCOMES** (but how do we know?). Questions of **PERSONHOOD** are logically prior to any other judgement.

## UTILITARIANS

**UTILITARIANS** seek to do an empirical calculation of good over evil (or pleasure/pain). **HEDONIC** utilitarians like Bentham balance pleasure/pain (eg emotional, financial, personal pleasure/pain). **RULE** utilitarians (Mill) calculate from past experience what social rules maximise happiness (eg the misery/death caused by backstreet abortions v happiness/misery of mothers having abortions). Rule utilitarians stress importance of **RIGHTS** and **JUSTICE**, but again, the question of whether the foetus is a person comes before we decide whether the mother's rights come before foetal rights. **PREFERENCE** utilitarians like **SINGER** might put more weight on a potential child's preferences, but in fact Singer's view of personhood (rational self-consciousness) allows for **INFANTICIDE** of disabled children.

## KANT

Kant argues for rational, a priori **UNIVERSALISABILITY** of autonomous (free) human beings. Again, question of **PERSONHOOD** comes first, otherwise we might discount the foetus completely and only universalise the mother's autonomous (free, self-legislating) choice. The **FORMULA OF ENDS** states we should never use human beings as just a means to an end, but as an end in themselves – with dignity, rights, and autonomy of their own. Abortion seems to break this formulation – but only if the foetus is a person. If the foetus is just like an appendix, there is arguably no moral issue for a Kantian.

# Euthanasia

## DEFINITIONS

**EUTHANASIA** (Greek = good death) is the practice of ending life to reduce pain and suffering (so "mercy killing").

**VOLUNTARY** euthanasia = when a patient's death is caused by another person eg doctor with the **EXPLICIT CONSENT** of the patient. The patient request must be **VOLUNTARY** (acting without coercion, pressure) **ENDURING** (lasts some time or is repeated over time) and **COMPETENT** (they have the mental capacity to choose). A variation on euthanasia is **PHYSICIAN-ASSISTED SUICIDE** – this differs from euthanasia as the doctor will help the patient to commit suicide (eg set up the apparatus), but the final act of killing is done by the patient.

**NON-VOLUNTARY** euthanasia is done **WITHOUT** the patient's consent, because they are not competent or able to give the consent (eg in a coma, on a life support machine). The doctor and/or the family may take the decision.

**INVOLUNTARY** euthanasia is performed **AGAINST** the wishes of the patient. This is widely opposed and illegal in the UK.

## ACTIVE OR PASSIVE

**ACTIVE** euthanasia is the **DIRECT** and **DELIBERATE** killing of a patient.

**PASSIVE** euthanasia is when life-sustaining treatment is withdrawn or withheld.

This distinction may also be described as the difference between an **ACT** and an **OMISSION** (failing to act) and between **KILLING** and **ALLOWING TO DIE**. Some, such as James Rachels, argue there is no real difference – if anything passive euthanasia (withdrawal of treatment) is worse because it leads to a longer, drawn out death and so more suffering potentially. **DAME CICELY SAUNDERS** (who founded the hospice movement) argues that it is unnecessary for anyone to suffer a painful death with modern drugs. A counter-argument is that many doctors already hasten death (eg by doubling a morphine dose): under the doctrine of **DOUBLE EFFECT** if the intention is to alleviate pain and a secondary effect to kill someone, the doctor is not guilty of any crime.

## LEGAL POSITION

Until 1961 suicide was illegal in the UK. The **1961 SUICIDE ACT** legalised suicide but made it illegal to assist.

The **NETHERLANDS** and **SWITZERLAND** allow voluntary euthanasia (active and passive) and physician-assisted suicide. The **DIGNITAS** clinic in Switzerland helped 107 British people to die in 2010. **DR ANNE TURNER** (aged 66) was one such person in 2009 – subject of the docu-drama "A Short Stay in Switzerland". No-one has ever been prosecuted in the UK for helping a relative or friend go to Switzerland.

In 2010 Director of Public Prosecutions **KEIR STARMER** confirmed that relatives of people who kill themselves will not face prosecution as long as they do not maliciously encourage them and assist only a "clear settled and informed wish" to commit suicide. The move came after the Law Lords backed multiple sclerosis sufferer Debbie Purdy's call for a policy statement on whether people who help someone commit suicide should be prosecuted. In August 2012 Tony Nicklinson, with "locked-in syndrome", failed in his legal attempt to end his "intolerable life"..

Keir Starmer concluded: "There are **NO GUARANTEES** against prosecution and it is my job to ensure that the most vulnerable people are protected while at the same time giving enough information to those people like Mrs Purdy who want to be able to make informed decisions about what actions they may choose to take".

The **OREGON RULES** are another attempt to legalise assisted suicide by laying down conditions under which it will be allowed in US law.

## SANCTITY OF LIFE: BIBLE

The Bible argues that life is a gift from God. Humans are created in the **IMAGE OF GOD** (Genesis 1:27) and the **INCARNATION** (God taking human form – John 1:14) shows the sacred value of human life. Human life is a **GIFT** or **LOAN** from God (Job 1:21 "The Lord gave and the Lord has taken away"). We should also show **RESPECT** for human life: "thou shalt not murder" (Exodus 20:13). We should also "choose life" (Deuteronomy 30). Finally, Christian love (**AGAPE**) is crucial (1 Corinthians 13 "the greatest value of all is love"). We should protect human life (the parable of the Good Samaritan) particularly as God gave his only son to redeem us (bring us back from sin and death) and give us the gift of "life in all its fullness".

# SANCTITY OF LIFE: NATURAL LAW

The **NATURAL LAW** view argues that there is a **PRIMARY PRECEPT** to "preserve life" and views life as an **INTRINSIC** good. Euthanasia is therefore wrong and the Catholic Church forbids both active and passive euthanasia as "contrary to the dignity of the human person and the respect due to God, his creator" (Catechism of the Roman Catholic Church). However, the **DOCTRINE OF DOUBLE EFFECT** might accept the shortening of human life (eg if the intention is to relieve pain, secondary effect to kill) so long as it is only a **FORESEEN BUT UNINTENDED RESULT**. The Catholic Church also makes a distinction between **ORDINARY** means (ordinary, usual medical treatments) and **EXTRAORDINARY** means (treatments that are dangerous, a huge burden, or disproportionate). It is morally acceptable to stop extraordinary means, as "it is the refusal of over-zealous treatment".

"Discontinuing medical procedures that are burdensome, dangerous, extraordinary, or disproportionate to the expected outcome can be legitimate; it is the refusal of "over-zealous" treatment. Here one does not will to cause death; one's inability to impede it is merely accepted. The decisions should be made by the patient if he is competent and able or, if not, by those legally entitled to act for the patient, whose reasonable will and legitimate interests must always be respected." Catechism 2278

# QUALITY OF LIFE

**JAMES RACHELS** argues that the sanctity of life tradition places too much value on human life and there are times (eg with abortion and euthanasia) when this is unhelpful. He makes a distinction between **BIOLOGICAL LIFE** ("being alive" = functioning biological organism) and **BIOGRAPHICAL LIFE** ("having a life" = everything that makes us who we are). He says that what matters is biographical life and if this is already over (for example in a **PERSISTENT VEGETATIVE STATE = PVS**), then taking away biological life is acceptable.

**PETER SINGER** argues that the worth of human life varies (the value of human life is not a sacred gift but depends on its **QUALITY**). A low quality of life (judged by the patient) can justify them taking their life or justify someone else doing it for them.

## AUTONOMY

**JOHN STUART MILL** (On Liberty, 1859) argues that individuals should have full **AUTONOMY** (the freedom to make decisions without coercion) so long as it does not harm other people. Individuals cannot be compelled to do things for their own good – "over his own mind-body the individual is sovereign". Those who support voluntary euthanasia believe that personal autonomy and self-determination (choosing what happens to you) are crucial. Any competent adult should be able to decide on the time and manner of their death.

**KANT** assumes autonomy as one of his three key postulates (with God and immortality). We are self-legislating, free moral beings. However, he argued in an essay on suicide that suicide was self-contradictory as, if it was universalised, the human race would die out.

## ARGUMENTS AGAINST EUTHANASIA

**PALLIATIVE CARE** – Dame Cicely Saunders argues that there is a better alternative for euthanasia in providing a pain-free death for terminally ill patients. The **HOSPICE** movement may be seen as an alternative, BUT , the euthanasia supporter might argue, this level of care is not available to everyone, is expensive and cannot fully relieve a patient's suffering (eg for someone who cannot breathe unassisted).

**VOLUNTARY AND COMPETENT** – some raise questions about voluntary euthanasia. Can the patient ever be free from coercion (eg relatives who want an inheritance or doctors who need to free up resources)? Is the patient likely to be competent (eg when under high doses of medication, or when depressed, or senile). Response would be that there are at least some clear cases when patients **ARE** clearly voluntary (not coerced) and competent. Guidelines such as Starmer's or the **OREGON RULES** require a certain time period of repeated requests to different people, which are then independently confirmed.

**SLIPPERY SLOPE** – this is the argument that once allowed, the outcome will be a process of a further decline in respect for human life and will end with the practice of non-voluntary euthanasia for the elderly seen as "unaffordable" by the working majority. A response might be that there is a clear difference between voluntary and non-voluntary euthanasia. Is there any evidence of a slippery slope in the state of Oregon or Switzerland? The rules on assisted suicide are drawn up precisely to stop the slide into widespread disrespect for human life.

**DOCTOR-PATIENT RELATIONSHIP** – some argue that doctors have a duty to preserve life (the **HIPPOCRATIC OATH**). Euthanasia will undermine the trust between patient and doctor if there is a fear that they will seek to end their life. However, as with abortion, there will remain doctors opposed to euthanasia which a patient could always choose, and it is highly unlikely that GPs will have any say in the process of mercy killing.

# Genetic Engineering

Genetic Engineering (**GE**) involves the practice of changing the genetic makeup of plants, animals or humans, or taking recombinant **DNA** (hybrid **DNA** made by artificially joining pieces of DNA from different sources) and using it for a special purpose. Novel reproductive technologies, such as those used in the cloning of sheep like Dolly, do not technically involve **GE**. A **GENE** is a sequence of **DNA** made up of just four chemical letters. There are approximately 24,000 genes in the human body. If all the **DNA** in all the cells in one person were stretched out they would reach to the moon and back 8,000 times. 20% of our genes are now **PATENTED** by those who discovered them. Similarly **GM SEED** is owned by the seed company that engineered it – and cannot be sown without their permission (or purchase).

## ISSUES

1. For what **PURPOSE** (making money? choosing eye colour? eliminating disease?).

2. With what **CONSEQUENCES** for biodiversity (plants) or human flourishing (**EUDAIMONIA**)?

3. Who decides? Do we as parents have the **RIGHT TO A CHILD** who is disease free? Is this an individual or social issue?

4. Should we **PLAY GOD** and manipulate nature?

5. Will a **SLIPPERY SLOPE** develop where one change leads to further unanticipated bad effects – such as the lowering of value of those with disabilities?

## PRESENT POSITION

The **GENOME** was fully sequenced by Craig Ventner by 2003 . Now it is possible to screen for genetic defects (**PRENATAL GENETIC DIAGNOSIS - PGD**) as part of IVF treatment, alter genetic makeup **IN UTERO** (in the uterus) and create **GENE THERAPIES** from **STEM CELLS** for potential treatment of various diseases. **DOLLY** the sheep was cloned in 1996 and had three parent sheep - one provided the egg, one the DNA and one the womb (though the South Korean scientist who claimed to have cloned humans proved to be a fraud). **CROPS** have been genetically modified by companies like **MONSANTO**.

## THE LAW

The **HUMAN FERTILITY AND EMBRYOLOGY ACT** (2008) established an authority for regulating genetic engineering in humans (the **HFEA**). **CLONING** is illegal unless a special **LICENCE** is obtained (first granted in 2004). Human and animal gametes can also be mixed (**NEWCASTLE UNIVERSITY**, 2006). **GENETIC ENGINEERING** of embryos is allowed in order to prevent a disability/ genetically inherited disease. **MULTIPLE** embryos can be fertilised – with issues of embryo wastage as the **BEST** are selected (shades of the wise men of Sparta selecting which baby lived or died). Or sperm can be injected directly into one egg – which most Christians find perfectly morally acceptable as no **WASTAGE** of embryos occurs. In the UK you cannot **DESIGN** a baby except for medical reasons – to create **SAVIOUR SIBLINGS** as in the film **MY SISTER's KEEPER**.

# UNNATURAL

Natural Law theory suggests we should not change the inviolable ousia (essence) or telos (goal) of any living organism. Both concepts come directly from Aristotelian philosophy. The GE of female turkeys to make them less broody (so that they lay more eggs), has been attacked by Jeremy **RIFKIN** as 'a serious violation of the intrinsic value of the creature'. RC Church argues that "a strictly therapeutic intervention whose explicit objective is the healing of various maladies such as those stemming from chromosomal defects will, in principle, be considered **DESIRABLE**, provided it is directed to the true promotion of the personal well-being of the individual without doing harm to his integrity or worsening his conditions of life". (Donum Vitae). But **CLONING** is absolutely prohibited, and embryo **WASTAGE** considered as evil as **ABORTION** – an assault on the **SANCTITY OF LIFE**.

# PLAYING GOD

Is GE good **STEWARDSHIP** or evil **DOMINION** (Genesis 1:26)? One-third of all agricultural production world-wide is lost to pests and diseases, and there is enormous scope for GE to render crops resistant to pests, drought and frost, to improve yields and to enable food to be produced in harsh environments. Some Christians argue we should use the new technology to feed a hungry world and to distribute its benefits more equitably. Others fear the consequences of upsetting biodiversity or exploiting poor farmers who are buying seed that they cannot resow next year. There is a evidence of a rise in suicide rates among Indian farmers who have been sold patented GM seed – is there a link?

# CONSEQUENCES

There are 5,000 inherited diseases which could be eliminated with mass genetic screening. Is this not a moral **GOOD**? Others argue that the **SANCTITY OF HUMAN LIFE** is violated and there will be **SOCIAL CONSEQUENCES** such as the change in perception about human suffering or the creation of a super-race (with two tiers of society like in the film **GATTACA**). To eliminate imperfections is to change the idea of being human, bowing to the **UTILITARIAN** argument that anything that produces human suffering is wrong, which many Christians reject due to the **REDEMPTIVE SUFFERING** of **JESUS** on the Cross.

# RIGHTS

Do I have the **RIGHT TO CHOOSE** the genetic makeup of a child? Or to have specially designed child to save another? Do I have a **DUTY** not to bring into the world a child who will suffer (perhaps in the same way as I did as a person with a genetic disease?)? Does a child have the **RIGHT TO KNOW** who are their genetic parents? Since 2005 the answer is "yes" – and sperm donor fathers have declined rapidly. Who has the right over a **SURROGATE** baby? Suppose the mother changes her mind? In America a famous case, the case of **BABY M**, involved a surrogate mother who changed her mind and refused to hand the baby over. The Catholic Church approves **GENETIC THERAPY** but disapproves strongly of **GENETIC ENHANCEMENT** where a child's characteristics are improved .

The production of human beings selected according to sex or other predetermined qualities, which change the genotype of the individual and of the human species, are contrary to the **PERSONAL DIGNITY** of the human being, to his integrity and to his identity. Therefore they can be in no way justified on the pretext that they will produce some beneficial results for humanity". Donum Vitae, Roman Catholic encyclical

Many people argue that GE opens a new era of **EUGENICS** so discredited by Nazi ideology, where genetic breeding is used to create a super-race.

## KANT

Kant's second formulation of the Categorical Imperative, the **PRINCIPLE OF ENDS** states that humans should never be treated just as a **MEANS** to an end but always an **END** in themselves. Designer babies and genetic enhancement seem to violate this principle. But what of **EMBRYO WASTAGE**?

It's not clear Kant would ever have accorded a collection of cells (whose gender etc was indeterminate) the **AUTONOMY** necessary to be human. If I knew I was going to be born with a genetic defect, would I choose to be born – applying **UNIVERSALISABILITY**? It seems clear that a **RATIONAL** human would choose to be born without a genetic disease.

Perhaps the Kantian answer continues to depend on the status we accord the **PRE-EMBRYO** (what doctors are starting to call an embryo up to 14 days old before the **PRIMITIVE STREAK** emerges).

# War & Pacifism

## JUST WAR THEORY

**JUST WAR THEORY (JWT)** is an attempt to provide conditions for **WHEN** war is acceptable and rules for **HOW** war should be conducted. It has its roots in Roman philosophy (especially **CICERO**), but was developed further by Christian theologians like **AUGUSTINE** (354-430) and then later by **AQUINAS** (1225-1274). Early Christians were **PACIFISTS** (based on Jesus' teaching such as "love your enemies" **MATTHEW** 5:44), but this situation changed after Constantine converted to Christianity after the **BATTLE OF MILVIAN BRIDGE** in 312 AD (as the Roman empire needed to defend itself against the northern tribes). JWT has three parts **JUS AD BELLUM** (literally "right to war" in Latin, so the morality of going to war), **JUS IN BELLO** (literally "right in war"), the moral rules conditions for fighting wars, and more recently in the twentieth century **JUS POST BELLUM** (right after war, or the moral rules for establishing a just peace after conflict).

## JUS AD BELLUM

**JUS AD BELLUM** describes six conditions for **WHEN** it is morally right to go to war.

1. **RIGHT AUTHORITY** – a state may only go to war if a decision is taken by an appropriate and legal authority.

2. **JUST CAUSE** – there must be a good reason for going to war = **INJUSTICE** = self-defence or defence of others, for example, UK treaty obligations to defend Poland in 1939.

3. **JUST INTENTION** – must go to war with the right intention or motive: Aquinas = "to promote good and avoid evil".

**FRANCISCO SUAREZ** and **FRANCISCO DE VITTORIA** (16th and 17th Century) added three more:

4. **LAST RESORT** – force can only be used when all other means of resolving the conflict have failed, for example, diplomacy and sanctions – such as sanctions on Iran and Syria in 2011.

5. **REASONABLE CHANCE OF SUCCESS** – deaths that happen in a hopeless cause are not morally justifiable.

6. **PROPORTIONALITY** – the benefits of waging war must be proportionate to the expected evils and harms caused eg don't go to war over fishing rights.

## JUS IN BELLO

**JUS IN BELLO** sets out three rules on how to conduct war:

1. **PROPORTIONALITY** – the methods used by soldiers must be proportionate: they should not be excessive to the ends they are seeking. For example, don't use an atomic bomb to enforce a UN resolution.

2. **CIVILIANS** – should never be directly targeted as happened in the Second World War in the bombing of Coventry or Dresden.

3. **MILITARY NECESSITY** – using the minimum force necessary to defeat the enemy: all military action must be necessary.

# JUS POST BELLUM

Brian **OREND** (The Morality of War) suggests the following principles:

1. **JUST CAUSE FOR TERMINATION** - A state may terminate a war if there has been a reasonable vindication of the rights that were violated in the first place, and if the aggressor is willing to negotiate the terms of surrender. These terms of surrender include a formal apology, compensations, war crimes trials and perhaps rehabilitation. Alternatively, a state may end a war if it becomes clear that any just goals of the war cannot be reached at all or cannot be reached without using excessive force.

2. **RIGHT INTENTION** - A state must only terminate a war under the conditions agreed upon in the above criteria. Revenge is not permitted. The victor state must also be willing to apply the same level of investigation into any war crimes its armed forces may have committed.

3. **PUBLIC DECLARATION AND AUTHORITY** - the terms of peace must be made by a legitimate authority, and the terms must be accepted by a legitimate authority.

4. **DISCRIMINATION** - the victor state is to differentiate between political and military leaders, and combatants and civilians. Punitive measures are to be limited to those directly responsible for the conflict.

5. **PROPORTIONALITY** - any terms of surrender must be proportional to the rights that were initially violated. Draconian measures or any attempt at denying the surrendered country the right to participate in the world community are not permitted.

## STRENGTHS OF JWT

1. Sets out clear **MORAL GUIDELINES** for going to war.

2. Influences the **BEHAVIOUR** of soldiers and politicians who may be brought before the International War Crimes Tribunal at the Hague (for example, the Bosnian war leaders).

3. It is **REALISTIC** – war is sometimes necessary to save lives and protect the innocent.

4. It is **UNIVERSAL** – and the basis for the work of the **UNITED NATIONS** and the **GENEVA CONVENTION**.

## WEAKNESSES

1. The **PERCEPTION** of the justice of war depends on a relative perspective, for example, the **US WAR ON TERROR** after the terrorist attack of 2001 led to the setting up of **GUANTANAMO BAY** detention centre in Cuba to hold people without trial. But the detention centre is arguably an unjust way of treating people in a war that is ill-defined (as wars against terrorists have to be).

2. The conditions are **AMBIGUOUS**. All wars involve the death of civilians (strangely called **COLLATERAL DAMAGE**) as it may be impossible to distinguish between a soldier and civilian.

3. It is **INAPPROPRIATE** for an age of terrorism when the aggrieved peoples (eg Palestinians) have **NO STATE** and hence are excluded from the ethics of just war theory which requires a legitimate authority. Are brutal states like **SYRIA** really a just authority? Who decides?

4.  Impossible to know the **CONSEQUENCES** and so we can only apply **JWT** looking backwards. Who would have agreed to the **IRAQ WAR** of 2003 had we known the level of casualties (mainly civilian – over one million Iraqis have died)?

## ABSOLUTE PACIFISM

**PACIFISTS** (Gandhi, Martin Luther King) argue violence is always wrong. It doesn't matter what the situation is. Violence should be met with a path of **PASSIVE RESISTANCE** (non-co-operation or even love of the enemy).

Reasons for absolute pacifism include:

1.  **JESUS'** teaching to "love your enemies" and "turn the other cheek" (meaning "never retaliate") in the **SERMON ON THE MOUNT** (Matthew 5) is echoed by **PAUL** who wrote: "Do not take revenge but leave room for God's wrath" (Romans 12:19) and gave the injunction to "repay evil with good".

2.  **QUAKERS** oppose war as they believe violence is destructive and builds a cycle of violence and revenge. The only way to break this cycle is the path of **AGAPE** love – to be prepared to sacrifice oneself for peace.

3.  **CONSCIENTIOUS OBJECTORS** refuse to fight wars on grounds of conscience. One famous objector was Bertrand Russell, who was imprisoned in 1916 for opposition to the war. "Fear has invaded our inmost being", he wrote.

# CRITICISMS OF ABSOLUTE PACIFISM

1. Fails to acknowledge **HUMAN SINFULNESS**. Reinhold **NIEBUHR** argued for **CHRISTIAN REALISM**: we cannot achieve ethical ideals (such as pacifism) because sin is present in everyone (especially self-interest and the desire to control others). Christians must sometimes use force to fight evil and establish **JUSTICE**. In the context of rising **FASCISM** war is an evil but necessary to prevent evils.

2. Fails to protect the **INNOCENT**. Elizabeth **ANSCOMBE** argues pacifism is immoral as it fails to protect the innocent and those who may suffer genocide. It denies the right of **SELF-DEFENCE**.

3. Failure to act (**OMISSION**) is as morally blameworthy as acting. **SINGER** and the utilitarians argue that consequences define the goodness and badness of an act so if we fail to stop eg the genocide in Bosnia we are morally culpable.

# CONTINGENT PACIFISM

Jonathan Glover (Causing Death, Saving Lives) is a **UTILITARIAN** who cannot adopt an **ABSOLUTIST** position. He does argue for a cultural shift away from war and because war rarely generates good consequences justification for war will be **RARE**.

Augustine was also a **CONTINGENT PACIFIST**, arguing that we cannot use violence to defend ourselves (turn the other cheek). But this counsel of perfection cannot apply to others. We do have the duty to protect the innocent in acts of **SELF-SACRIFICE**.

# The Four Questions Answered

In the first section of this book I mentioned that there are four questions we need to ask of any moral theory. They spell the acronym **DARM** (**D**erivation, **A**pplication, **R**ealism, **M**otivation).

## 1. HOW IS THE IDEA OF GOODNESS DERIVED?

Goodness has to come from somewhere – it is, after all a human construct. The normal candidates are three:

1. God

2. Reason

3. Observation or experience.

**RELATIVISTS** argue that our idea of goodness comes directly from **CULTURE** (what JL Mackie in Inventing Right and Wrong calls "forms of life") or from **EXPERIENCE** (the utilitarian or situationist view that we judge right and wrong according to circumstances and likely consequences).

**NATURAL LAW** theorists like **AQUINAS** argue that goodness is partly an **A PRIORI** idea given by God – what he calls synderesis "the intuitive knowledge of first principles", and partly an **A POSTERIORI** idea worked out by experience as we develop our conscience and practical wisdom by looking at circumstances . Natural Law goods are in the end **OBSERVABLE GOODS**. We apply the **PRIMARY PRECEPTS** (acronym **POWER**) to situations.

**KANT** argues that morality is an **A PRIORI** category of the mind like number or cause and effect. Just as we need a concept of **NUMBER** before we can count, so we need a concept of the **CATEGORICAL IMPERATIVE** before we can apply it to the world and synthetic experience where we discover how it works. Morality is therefore **A PRIORI SYNTHETIC**.

**UTLITARIANS** see goodness as a **TELEOLOGICAL** idea depending on the end we pursue, either **PLEASURE** (the psychological "sovereign two masters, pleasure and pain" of Bentham) or **HAPPINESS** (it is good because most people desire it as an end in itself, says **MILL**). So goodness is measurable, an **OBJECTIVE, EMPIRICAL IDEA**, either by counting **HEDONS** (Bentham) or **DESIRES** (Mill). This is therefore a theory appealing to **A POSTERIORI** knowledge because we cannot know consequences without some experience of them.

**DIVINE COMMAND THEORISTS** argue that God has revealed the moral law to us in **SCRIPTURE** which has commands like the ten commandments which we need to understand and then obey. We have an **INNATE** conscience, as St Paul argues we all (believer or non-believer) have "the law written on our hearts" (Romans 2:15). This implies **A PRIORI** God-given knowledge of good and evil.

Notice that only two of these theories are purely **DEONTOLOGICAL**, Kantian ethics and Divine Command Theory. **NATURAL LAW** has deontological outcomes (the **SECONDARY PRECEPTS**) which come from a **TELEOLOGICAL WORLDVIEW** because in Natural law everything has a proper rational purpose (**TELOS**).

# 2. HOW ARE THE THEORIES APPLIED?

**RELATIVISTS** see goodness as relative to culture or experience and so any situation needs to be applied to the relevant cultural value. These may still be very **REASONABLE** but, argues the relativist, even **REASON** is culturally conditioned and not **PURE** as Kant implied.

**NATURAL LAW THEORY** applies the five primary precepts (acronym **POWER**) to produce the secondary precepts. So the **P** of **POWER** (preservation of life) yields the **SECONDARY PRECEPT** do not abort, do not commit suicide, do not murder. These are not **ABSOLUTE RULES** as we allow killing in time of war. Ultimately the primary precepts are derived from a socially relative idea of **HUMAN FLOURISHING** – what it means for a human being to live well or excellently.

**KANT** sees right and wrong as something irrational, a **CONTRADICTION** or logical inconsistency. There are two types of self contradiction: the **CONTRADICTION IN NATURE** includes suicide and breaking your promises. These cannot be willed universally without contradiction because **EUTHANASIA** if universalised leads to mass suicide of those in pain, and breaking your promise if universalised leads to the elimination of the idea of promising altogether. A **CONTRADICTION IN WILL** is not illogical, but cannot be universally willed or desired. We could never desire not to help our neighbour in distress because we would always want to be helped when we are in distress.

**UTILITARIANS** see the right action as one that maximises happiness or pleasure. So we need to examine the likely consequences, count how many are affected by our choice, and then apply the Greatest Happiness Principle. We apply utilitarian principles **CONSEQUENTIALLY**.

However, utilitarians still have the challenge of explaining why I should have a **DUTY** to consider the interests or happiness of others (even complete strangers) in my utilitarian calculation. Can utilitarian ethics escape from this essential **EGOISM** and partiality - that my happiness or possibly mine and my family's has greater weight than the **GENERAL** happiness. Is **SINGER**'s universal objective viewpoint which assesses perferences of all affected by my action really possible or even desirable?

**DIVINE COMMAND THEORISTS** argue that we should obey God's commands because God is good. He is the source of goodness (holiness, perfection) and love (to a Christian this means **AGAPE** love or sacrificial love for the stranger). So anything he wills and commands must be good. We should not question God: just find a Bible verse that is relevant and apply it.

# 3. REALISM

How realistic are these theories from the perspective of modern sciences such as **PSYCHOLOGY** and **BIOLOGY**?

**RELATIVISM** fits well the postmodern world where there is no one overarching narrative accepted as true. It also fits **FREUDIAN** psychology where conscience comes from our upbringing and the sense of shame engendered by our parents and teachers. In the postmodern age we are taught to **TOLERATE** difference.

**NATURAL LAW** is often condemned as outdated. However the idea of a shared rational nature is something evolutionary biologists accept. **RICHARD DAWKINS** (The Selfish Gene) talks of a "lust to be nice" coming from our evolved sense of obligation to one another. Is this so different from **AQUINAS'** synderesis principle that we by nature "do good and avoid evil"? Dawkins rejects the **TELEOLOGICAL** nature of Natural Law, as there is no purpose to **EVOLUTION**, he argues, just an endless struggle to survive. But we have inherited an **ALTRUISTIC GENE** from this battle of the genes giving us a shared moral nature. The selfish gene is the self-promoting gene, but for humans, it is in our interest to be moral and so, argues Dawkins, the selfish gene gives us our moral sense and desire to help others.

**KANT'S** ethical theory can be criticised for being **DUALISTIC**. So he sees the world of experience, the **PHENOMENAL** world as opposed to the world of ideas, the **NOUMENAL** world. He also contrasts **REASON** and **EMOTION** in a way that seems to deny moral worth to an action done out of compassion rather than duty alone. The outcome of his theory, that categorical rules are **ABSOLUTE** can also be criticised as unrealistic. In practice we do lie to save someone's life – the goodness is situational, not absolute as Kant suggests.

**DIVINE COMMAND THEORY** suggests I can read God's commands from a Holy Book and then apply them easily to the present day. But this is unrealistic. The Bible says nothing about abortion, euthanasia, just war principles, or genetic engineering. So we have to interpret and extrapolate. What exactly did Paul mean by "women should keep silent in church" (1 Corinthians 14:33)? If we reject parts of Leviticus as no longer applying (stoning the adulterer for example) then what about other parts of the Bible? How do we decide? How should we extrapolate (extend) the principle "thou shalt not kill" (Exodus 20:13)? This seems to include a prior question - who or what has an absolute right to life (embryo, foetus, person on life support machine, soldier in war, civilian in war etc)?

# 4. MOTIVATION: WHY BE MORAL?

So we come to the final, and perhaps most pressing question. Why be moral at all? Why not live a life of selfish egoism and be a parasite on the goodness of everyone else?

**RELATIVISM** is a wide and ambiguous concept. Joseph Fletcher (Situation Ethics) defined himself as a relativist (Situation Ethics is a form of **CHRISTIAN** relativism). He argued that we are moral out of love for fellow human beings. But this begs the question why I should bother about fellow human beings when it's not in my interest to do so. Fletcher's answer was that we need to convert to the way of love - commitment comes before action. He calls this **THEOLOGICAL POSITIVISM**. Situation ethics is something of a special case and is arguably not a pure form of relativism as it has one **ABSOLUTE** at its centre - agape love.

**NATURAL LAW** theorists argue from a **TELEOLOGICAL** standpoint. Be moral, they say, because it is reasonable to want to flourish as a human being – to be the most excellent person you can be. A knife should cut well, says Aristotle, and a human being should be rational in order to flourish well. **AQUINAS** argues that our greatest happiness will be found by aligning the natural law with God's eternal law. This will cause us to be a full, complete human being.

**KANT** takes the stern, dutiful line of obedience to the moral law or **CATEGORICAL IMPERATIVE**. He argues that rational people will freely choose this way as the most logically consistent way of arriving at the **SUMMUM BONUM**, the greatest good. Autonomous human beings will realise that to obey the categorical imperative out of duty is the best way of building the best of all conceivable moral worlds. Like Kant himself, this moral law within should fill us with awe. It's wonderful. The summum bonum is a mixture of virtue (dutifulness) and happiness ultimately only discovered in heaven (Kant's postulate of **IMMORTALITY**).

**UTILITARIANS** are not agreed on what motivates us. **BENTHAM** thought we were psychological **HEDONISTS** motivated by the prospect of pleasure and avoiding pain. **MILL** disagreed. He thought pleasure and happiness were not the same, as happiness needed clear goals and strenuous activities. Happiness is to be found in challenges met and difficulties overcome – which sometimes can involve discipline and sacrifice. Why bother with the happiness of others? Mill answered, out of **SYMPATHY** for my fellow human beings. "In the Golden Rule of Jesus of Nazareth ("do to others as you would have them do to you" Matthew 7:18)", wrote Mill, "is all the ethics of utility".

**DIVINE COMMAND THEORY** argues for two motivations – love of God and fear of God. We should love God because he created us and first loved us and redeemed us by his Son. And we should fear him because he is holy and just and will one day judge us, as the **PARABLE OF THE SHEEP AND GOATS** suggests, according to how we have treated the poor, needy, homeless and vulnerable. "As you have done to the least of these, you have also done to me", says Jesus. Failure to love and obey God, if the same parable is believed will result in "eternal punishment", not "eternal life" (Matthew 25:45,46).

# Exam Rescue Remedy

1. Build your own scaffolding which represents the logic of the theory. Use a mind map or a summary sheet.

2. Do an analysis of past questions by theme as well as by year (see philosophicalinvestigations.co.uk website for examples). Try writing your own Philosophy of Religion paper based on what hasn't come up recently.

3. Examine examiners' reports (go to their website) for clues as to how to answer a question well.

4. Use the **AREA** approach suggested in this revision guide. **ARGUMENT**- Have I explained the argument (from Plato or Kant for example)? **RESPONSE** - Have I outlined and explained a good range of responses to the argument? **EVALUATION** - Now I have clearly set out positions, what do I think of these? Is mine **A PHILOSOPHICAL** argument and why. Does the original argument stand or fall against the criticisms raised? Why or why not?

5. List relevant technical vocabulary for inclusion in essay (eg efficient cause, form of the good, analytic, synthetic).

6. Prepare key quotes from selected key authors, original/ contemporary (eg quotes list from the A level website philosophicalinvestigations.co.uk – even better, produce your own). Learn some.

7. Contrast and then evaluate different views/theories/authors as

some questions ask "which approach is best?" So contrast every approach with one other and decide beforehand what you think.

8. Practise writing for 35 minutes. Don't use a computer, unless you do so in the exam.

9. Always answer and discuss the exact question in front of you, never learn a "model answer". Use your own examples (newspapers, films, documentaries, real life). Be prepared to think creatively and adapt your knowledge to the question.

10. Conclude with your view, justify it (give reasons) especially with "discuss".

# Postscript

Peter Baron taught Religious Studies at Wells Cathedral School from 2006-12, and before that taught Economics and Politics at Tonbridge School in Kent (1982-1991). He currently works as a freelance speaker and writer and is producing a series of books on ethics to be published in the autumn of 2012.

This revision guide is based on detailed handouts and powerpoints on the author's website. A teacher's guide is being prepared with detailed powerpoints, games, templates, and activities. Please consult the website for further details.

Students seeking fuller explanations and a bibliography should also consult the website which also contains exam tips and past questions listed by theme.

The author welcomes comments on the Revision Guide and contributions to the website - details are to be found online at:

**www.philosophicalinvestigations.co.uk**

Lightning Source UK Ltd.
Milton Keynes UK
UKOW05f1243130315

247817UK00001B/39/P

9 781909 618046